# HOW TO START SIDE HUSTLE BUSINESS

*A Proven 5-Step Blueprint for Building, Scaling, and Automating Your Lucrative Side Hustle to Achieve Long-Term Wealth*

## Jerry R. Schaefer

Copyright © 2024 By [ Jerry R. Schaefer]

All content in this book is protected under copyright laws. Any reproduction, distribution, or unauthorized use of any part of this book without the prior written consent of the copyright owner is strictly prohibited except for personal use.

## OTHER BOOKS BY SAME AUTHOR

1. HOW TO INVEST FOR EARLY RETIREMENT
2. LIVING THE FRUGAL MINDSET
3. HOW TO START AN AIRBNB BUSINESS AS A BUSINESS
4. THE ULTIMATE BUSINESS STORYTELLING GUIDE
5. HOW TO START FOOD TRUCK BUSINESS
6. HOW TO GROW SMALL BUSINESS
7. HOW TO FLIP HOUSES FOR BEGINNERS
8. HOW TO INVEST FOR TEENAGERS
9. HOW TO INVEST $10,000 INTO FINANCIAL FREEDOM

# TABLE OF CONTENTS

# Introduction

In a world where the traditional career trajectory is being redefined, the concept of a side hustle has emerged as a beacon of financial empowerment and independence. Gone are the days when individuals relied solely on a 9-to-5 job for income; the contemporary landscape encourages the cultivation of additional streams of revenue through side hustles. The allure of creating one's path to financial freedom and breaking free from the chains of a paycheck-to-paycheck existence has fueled the rise of side hustles.

But what exactly is a side hustle, and why has it become such a buzzword in today's dynamic economy?

A side hustle, at its core, is a supplementary income-generating activity pursued alongside a full-time job or other primary commitments. It's not just a fleeting trend; it's a mindset shift, a way of thinking that empowers individuals to take control of their financial destinies. The allure of a side hustle lies in its flexibility, adaptability, and the potential for exponential growth beyond the constraints of a traditional job.

In this journey towards mastering the art of the side hustle, we'll navigate through the misconceptions that often surround the topic. You might have heard people proclaiming that dropshipping is dead, or that affiliate marketing is too hard, while others argue that significant capital is a prerequisite for starting a side hustle. Let's debunk these myths and uncover the truth—they aren't dead or too hard; the challenge lies in the competitiveness and the misconception that substantial funds are mandatory.

This exploration is not a promise of an effortless formula for success. If you're seeking a shortcut or a get-rich-quick scheme, you won't find it here—or anywhere else, for that matter. What we offer is a practical, step-by-step guide grounded in real experiences, the kind that took years of dedication and hard work to become a reality.

**The Side Hustle as a Video Game**

Embarking on a side hustle is akin to playing a strategic video game. Just like in a game where you level up your character's power, in the realm of side hustles, you enhance your capabilities through assimilating knowledge and developing valuable skills. However, unlike a game, your real-life avatar doesn't come pre-equipped with skills or a ready-made six-pack. It requires dedication, effort, and a commitment to acquiring valuable skills that a sizable market is willing to pay for in the future.

Crucially, the emphasis here is on becoming "good enough" rather than striving for expert status. Spending years trying to attain expertise before earning money is counterproductive. The focus is on efficiently acquiring skills and putting them into action, understanding that perfection is not a prerequisite for profitability.

**Challenging Traditional Education Narratives**

In a society that often places a high value on traditional education, we challenge the notion that paying for conventional education is the only path to success. While knowledge undoubtedly holds power, the necessity of traditional education, especially if your goal is a non-traditional career path, is questioned. Learning a skill while actively making money becomes a compelling alternative—one that aligns with the ethos of this side hustle mastery journey.

Consider the story of someone like a counselor who felt compelled to accumulate more qualifications before charging for services. The realization that expertise is not solely tied to formal qualifications opens up avenues for faster entry into the market, helping individuals actively get paid for their skills sooner.

**Choosing Your Skill and Overcoming Mental Blocks**

The pivotal moment in your side hustle journey arrives when you decide what skill you want to learn. However, it's not just about any skill; it needs to have a broad enough appeal to attract potential clients. The urgency to act now, instead of waiting for years to perfect a skill, is emphasized. There are people out there who need your skills at this moment, not years down the line.

The narrative challenges the complacency of those with ample free time who choose not to invest it in acquiring new skills. While relaxation is valid, the frustration emerges when people complain about their situations without taking action to change them. Society, often geared towards a docile population, encourages conformity and discourages initiative. The call here is to break free from this mold and actively pursue skills that can reshape your financial destiny.

**Untapped Side Hustle Ideas**

The world is rife with side hustle opportunities, from video creation, coding, and negotiation to practical trades like carpentry and plumbing. The key is to identify a skill, learn it, and position yourself in the market. Whether it's coding, physical trades, or video editing, there are avenues to be handsomely paid for leveling up your avatar.

This introduction sets the stage for the journey ahead—a journey into the realm of side hustle mastery, where dedication, skill development, and strategic planning converge to unlock the doors to financial independence. The subsequent steps will unravel the blueprint for success, guiding you through the intricate process of building, scaling, and automating a side hustle that goes beyond a mere supplementary income to become a sustainable and lucrative venture.

# Dispelling Common Myths: Unmasking the Truth About Side Hustles

In the realm of side hustles, there exists a tapestry of myths that can deter aspiring entrepreneurs. It's crucial to dispel these misconceptions to pave the way for a clearer understanding of the journey ahead.

## Myth 1: Dropshipping is Dead

Contrary to the proclamation that dropshipping has met its demise, the reality is that it has evolved. While the landscape may be more competitive, the demise is overstated. Success in dropshipping, like any side hustle, requires adaptability, effective marketing strategies, and a keen understanding of market trends.

## Myth 2: Affiliate Marketing is Too Hard

Affiliate marketing is often deemed challenging, but the difficulty lies in the misconception that success is instantaneous. It demands patience, consistent effort, and strategic marketing. With the right approach and understanding of the target audience, affiliate marketing can be a lucrative avenue for passive income.

**Myth 3: Needing Money to Start**

The belief that significant capital is a prerequisite for a side hustle is a pervasive myth. While some ventures may require initial investment, many successful entrepreneurs started with minimal funds. The emphasis should be on resourcefulness, creativity, and leveraging available tools and platforms.

**Myth 4: Quick and Easy Formula to Success**

The idea that a quick and easy formula guarantees success is a fallacy. Side hustle mastery is a journey that demands dedication, hard work, and a willingness to learn from both successes and failures. There is no one-size-fits-all solution; success is forged through continuous refinement and adaptation.

**Myth 5: Side Hustles are Too Competitive**

While it's true that the side hustle landscape is competitive, framing it as an insurmountable obstacle undermines the potential for success. The key is to identify a niche, offer a standout service, and continuously innovate. A well-positioned side hustle can thrive even in a competitive market.

By dispelling these myths, aspiring entrepreneurs can approach the world of side hustles with a realistic mindset, understanding that challenges are part of the journey. The subsequent steps will illuminate the path to success, offering actionable strategies to navigate and conquer the intricacies of building a thriving side hustle.

# Step 1: Develop Skills

## The Video Game Analogy: Increasing Your Character's Power

Embarking on the journey of a side hustle is akin to entering a dynamic video game. Just as a player must level up their character's power to navigate challenges, in the world of side hustles, the equivalent power-up is the development of valuable skills. This step lays the foundation for success, emphasizing the importance of acquiring skills that resonate with a broad market.

Imagine your side hustle journey as a strategic video game. Initially, your character is a novice, lacking the skills needed to thrive in the competitive landscape. Much like a player seeks to increase their character's abilities, you must assimilate knowledge and cultivate skills to elevate your prowess in the realm of side hustles.

The analogy underscores the need for dedication and continuous improvement, mirroring the progression of a character in a game. Instead of waiting to become an expert, the focus is on becoming "good enough" to offer value and start earning. This approach counters the misconception that years of expertise are prerequisites for making money—a fallacy that can hinder early progress.

A valuable skill, in this context, is anything you can learn that a sizable market is willing to pay for in the future. The emphasis on becoming proficient rather than an expert allows for a quicker entry into the market. The analogy encourages aspiring entrepreneurs to view skill development as a gradual power-up process, where each acquired skill contributes to an overall increase in market value.

In essence, Step 1 is a call to action—a commitment to leveling up your avatar by dedicating time and effort to acquire skills that position you as a valuable player in the expansive landscape of side hustles. This step sets the tone for the journey ahead, highlighting the importance of continuous learning, adaptability, and a proactive approach to skill development in the evolving world of side hustles.

## Becoming Good Enough vs. Striving for Expertise

In the pursuit of side hustle mastery, a crucial distinction emerges between the pursuit of becoming "good enough" and the traditional notion of striving for expertise. This strategic approach challenges the conventional wisdom that success is contingent on years of becoming an absolute authority in a particular field.

The essence of becoming "good enough" lies in recognizing the diminishing returns associated with prolonged efforts to achieve expertise. While expertise is valuable in certain contexts, it often comes at the cost of delayed entry into the market and missed opportunities for early monetization. The emphasis shifts from perfection to proficiency, allowing individuals to start earning and refining their skills in real-world scenarios.

Striving for expertise can inadvertently become a barrier to entry for many aspiring entrepreneurs. It implies a prolonged period of dedication solely to the pursuit of knowledge without immediate application. This traditional approach, often associated with formal education, may not align with the dynamic nature of side hustles, where adaptability and swift execution play pivotal roles.

The "good enough" philosophy encourages a pragmatic mindset—one that recognizes the importance of continuously learning and evolving in response to market demands. It advocates for acquiring the necessary skills to offer value without getting bogged down by the unrealistic pursuit of perfection. This approach aligns with the fast-paced nature of the digital age, where agility and versatility often outweigh a deep but narrow expertise.

Moreover, the strategic decision to become "good enough" positions individuals as early contributors to the market. It allows for the development of a feedback loop, enabling entrepreneurs to refine their skills based on real-world experiences and market responses. This iterative process not only accelerates personal growth but also cultivates a mindset of resilience and adaptability—essential traits in the ever-changing landscape of side hustles.

In essence, the choice between becoming "good enough" and striving for expertise is a pivotal one in the journey towards side hustle mastery. The strategic entrepreneur understands the value of timely action, leveraging proficiency as a catalyst for early success, and embracing a continuous learning mindset as the foundation for sustained growth.

## Learning While Making Money: The Value of Skill Acquisition

In the realm of side hustle mastery, a paradigm shift is occurring—one that challenges the traditional trajectory of extensive education before entering the market. Central to this shift is the concept of learning while actively making money, a dynamic approach that emphasizes the simultaneous acquisition of skills and income generation.

The traditional narrative often dictates that one must invest substantial time and financial resources in formal education before venturing into the professional arena. However, the emerging ethos of side hustle mastery challenges this norm, advocating for a more pragmatic path—one where individuals learn valuable skills while actively participating in the market.

This approach recognizes that the most impactful learning occurs through hands-on experiences and real-world application. It positions the side hustler as an active participant in their own education, learning and adapting in response to the challenges and opportunities presented by their ventures. In essence, the side hustler becomes both the student and the entrepreneur, navigating the intricate landscape of skill acquisition while simultaneously building a source of income.

The value of skill acquisition is twofold in this context. First and foremost, it enables individuals to offer tangible value to potential clients or customers. Whether it's coding, video editing, graphic design, or any other skill with market demand, the ability to provide a service becomes the foundation for income generation. This aligns with the core philosophy of the side hustle—taking action and delivering value from the outset.

Secondly, learning while making money cultivates a mindset of adaptability and resilience. The side hustler becomes adept at navigating the uncertainties of the market, iterating on their skills based on real-world feedback, and continuously improving to meet evolving demands. This iterative process of skill acquisition becomes a dynamic cycle, propelling the entrepreneur forward on their journey to mastery.

In conclusion, the value of skill acquisition in side hustle mastery lies not only in the immediate income generation but also in the development of a versatile and adaptable mindset. Learning while making money transcends the confines of traditional education, empowering individuals to forge their paths to success through active participation, continuous learning, and the strategic application of acquired skills.

# Step 2: Offer a Standout Service - Niche Positioning: Becoming an Expert in Your Field

As the journey towards side hustle mastery unfolds, Step 2 catapults entrepreneurs into the realm of offering a standout service. Central to this step is the strategic concept of niche positioning—crafting a unique identity in a specific area, becoming not just a service provider but an expert within a defined field.

**Niche Positioning as the Cornerstone:**

Niche positioning is the art of honing in on a specific segment of the market where your skills and expertise can shine brightly. Instead of being a generalist, spreading efforts thinly across various domains, niche positioning encourages entrepreneurs to become specialists in a particular field. This specialization not only differentiates you from the competition but also allows you to be perceived as an authority, a go-to expert in your chosen niche.

**Expertise Over Jack-of-All-Trades:**

In a world brimming with options, being perceived as a specialist holds unparalleled value. The truth is, while a generalist might possess a broad range of skills, they may not be perceived as adept or authoritative in any single area. Niche positioning counters this by elevating you to a status beyond a mere service provider—you become the expert that clients seek out for specialized solutions.

**Choosing Your Niche:**

Selecting the right niche involves a careful evaluation of two crucial factors: earning potential and personal enjoyment. The ideal scenario is finding a niche where your skills align with market demands, ensuring a steady stream of clients willing to pay for your expertise. However, personal fulfillment is equally vital; pursuing a niche solely for financial gain may lead to burnout. Striking a balance between financial viability and personal enjoyment is key to sustained success.

**Breaking Through the Noise:**

In a world inundated with choices, standing out is imperative. Niche positioning is the antidote to being lost in the crowd. It allows you to tailor your services to a specific audience, addressing their unique needs with precision. By doing so, you not only become the preferred choice but also mitigate the pressure of price competition—clients are willing to pay a premium for specialized expertise.

In essence, Step 2 urges aspiring entrepreneurs to transcend the conventional role of a service provider and embrace the mantle of an expert within a niche. Niche positioning is not just about narrowing focus; it's about amplifying impact, fostering client trust, and ultimately building a standout service that becomes the cornerstone of your side hustle success.

## Financial Incentives: Making More Money for Your Clients

Step 2 of the side hustle mastery journey unfolds a strategic layer that goes beyond merely providing a service—it's about creating financial incentives that not only benefit you but, more crucially, make more money for your clients. The concept of financial incentives transforms your role from a service provider to a value-driven partner, aligning your success with the success of those you serve.

Shifting the Focus:

Traditionally, the emphasis in business has often been on the product or service offered. However, the paradigm shift advocated in Step 2 places the spotlight on the financial benefits your service brings to your clients. It's not about the product itself; it's about how that product translates into tangible financial gains for those who invest in it.

**Selling the Outcome, Not the Output:**

In the realm of financial incentives, the approach shifts from selling the output (the service or product) to selling the outcome—the positive impact that your service will have on the client's bottom line. This reframing is crucial as clients are ultimately concerned with how your offerings will contribute to their financial success rather than the intricacies of the service itself.

**Understanding Client Needs:**

To create effective financial incentives, a deep understanding of your client's business and objectives is paramount. What are their pain points, and how can your service alleviate them? What financial goals are they aiming to achieve, and how can your expertise contribute to their success? Tailoring your services to directly address these needs ensures that the financial incentives you offer are both meaningful and impactful.

**Articulating the Value Proposition:**

Communicating the financial incentives effectively becomes a skill in itself. It involves articulating a compelling value proposition that clearly demonstrates how your service will enhance your client's financial standing. Whether it's through increased revenue, cost savings, or efficiency gains, the value proposition should resonate with the client's overarching financial goals.

**Building Long-Term Partnerships:**

By aligning your success with the financial success of your clients, you foster a foundation for long-term partnerships. It's a symbiotic relationship where both parties thrive. Your clients benefit not only from the immediate value of your service but also from the continuous financial gains facilitated by your expertise.

In conclusion, financial incentives elevate your role as a side hustler to that of a strategic partner. It's about understanding the financial landscape of your clients, crafting solutions that directly contribute to their success, and ultimately creating a side hustle that transcends the transactional to become an indispensable asset in the financial journey of those you serve.

## Skill Stacking: Creating a Unique Service Package

Step 2 propels entrepreneurs into the realm of offering a standout service, and within this step, the concept of skill stacking emerges as a powerful strategy for crafting a unique service package. Skill stacking involves combining a diverse set of valuable skills acquired in Step 1 and synergizing them into a cohesive offering that sets you apart in the competitive landscape of side hustles.

**The Jigsaw Puzzle of Skills:**

Imagine your skillset as a collection of puzzle pieces—each skill acquired in Step 1 is a piece that contributes to the overall picture. Skill stacking involves strategically combining these pieces to create a comprehensive service package that goes beyond individual capabilities. It's about recognizing the synergy between different skills and leveraging them collectively for maximum impact.

**Niche Expertise Through Skill Stacking:**

Skill stacking enables you to position yourself as a niche expert by addressing multiple facets of a client's needs. Instead of offering isolated services, you become a one-stop solution that can navigate various challenges. This comprehensive approach not only adds value to your services but also reinforces your status as a specialized authority within your chosen niche.

**The Three Pillars of Skill Stacking:**

Breaking down skill stacking, it comprises three essential pillars:

Niche Specialization: Focus on a specific niche within your industry where your skill stack can have the most significant impact. Whether it's social media strategy, video production, or web development, tailor your stack to cater to the unique needs of your chosen niche.

Financial Incentive Expertise: Infuse your skill stack with the ability to create financial incentives for your clients. Understand how your combined skills can directly contribute to their financial success, and articulate this value proposition effectively.

Adaptability: The beauty of skill stacking lies in its adaptability. As the market evolves, your skill stack can evolve with it. Stay attuned to industry trends and continuously refine your stack to remain a dynamic force in your niche.

**Crafting Your Standout Offer:**

Skill stacking is about more than technical proficiency; it's about crafting a service package that is greater than the sum of its parts. By combining niche expertise, financial incentive acumen, and adaptability, you create a standout offer that not only addresses the current needs of the market but also evolves to meet future challenges.

In essence, skill stacking is the strategic art of weaving together your acquired skills into a unique service package. It's about going beyond individual competencies, creating a holistic offering, and positioning yourself as the go-to expert within your specialized niche.

# Step 3: Productize Your Service

## The Power of Scalability: Transforming Services into Products

As the journey towards side hustle mastery advances, Step 3 introduces a game-changing strategy—productizing your service. This step involves the transformation of your service offerings into tangible products with a focus on scalability. The power of scalability not only expands your reach but also allows you to serve a broader audience without an exponential increase in hands-on work for each project.

**Unleashing the Potential of Productization:**

Productizing your service is akin to unlocking a new level in the side hustle game. It involves outlining precisely what your customers will receive and at what price, enabling you to sell this standardized product to multiple clients. The shift from bespoke services to productized offerings introduces predictability, repeatability, and efficiency into your side hustle model.

**Scalability Defined:**

At the core of this step lies the concept of scalability—the ability to handle an increasing workload or demand without compromising efficiency. Productization enables side hustlers to scale their operations by streamlining processes and delivering standardized services. It's about finding the balance between maintaining quality and accommodating a growing clientele.

**The Model of Repeatable Success:**

A productized service is designed to be repeatable with minimal modifications required for different clients or projects. This repeatability fosters a streamlined workflow, allowing you to efficiently serve multiple customers without reinventing the wheel for each project. The model becomes a template for success that can be applied across various scenarios, creating a framework for consistent delivery.

**Crafting Your Productized Service:**

To embark on the journey of productization, you need to outline precisely what your customers will receive. This involves breaking down your service into components, defining the scope, and establishing a clear pricing structure. The goal is to create a standardized product that can be easily communicated and understood by potential clients.

**Expanding Reach Through Online Platforms:**

Productizing services aligns seamlessly with the digital age, where online platforms provide a gateway to a global audience. Leveraging websites, marketplaces, or dedicated platforms for your productized service enables you to reach clients beyond geographical constraints. The online realm becomes the marketplace for your standardized offerings, opening doors to a diverse clientele.

**Realizing the Efficiency Gains:**

One of the primary advantages of productization is the efficiency gains it offers. By standardizing your service into a product, you reduce the need for custom solutions for each client, saving time and effort. This efficiency translates into the ability to handle a higher volume of projects simultaneously, maximizing your earning potential.

## Case in Point: Online Courses and Done-for-You Packages:

Two prominent examples of productized services are online courses and done-for-you packages. Online courses, created once and accessible to a multitude of users, showcase the scalability inherent in productization. Similarly, done-for-you packages in web design, content creation, or coaching courses follow a standardized process, allowing side hustlers to serve numerous clients without starting from scratch for each project.

## Adapting to Different Clients:

While the productized service is standardized, there is room for adaptation to meet the unique needs of different clients. This adaptability ensures that the core offering remains consistent while allowing for minor modifications to cater to specific requirements. The key is to strike a balance between standardization and flexibility.

In conclusion, Step 3 introduces the transformative power of scalability through productizing your service. By converting your offerings into standardized products, you create a framework for repeatable success, maximize efficiency, and expand your reach to a global audience. The strategic shift from bespoke services to productized offerings propels your side hustle towards a new realm of growth and profitability.

## Outlining and Pricing Your Productized Service

In the journey of productizing your service, the pivotal steps of outlining and pricing are where the strategic blueprint for success takes shape. This phase involves breaking down your service into clear components, defining the scope of your offering, and establishing a pricing structure that not only reflects the value you provide but also appeals to your target audience.

**Comprehensive Outlining:**

The process of outlining your productized service is akin to creating a roadmap for your clients. It requires a meticulous examination of your service components, identifying the key features, and defining the deliverables. Think of it as crafting a user manual for your offering—one that clearly communicates what clients can expect to receive, ensuring transparency and setting realistic expectations.

**Defining Scope with Precision:**

Precision in defining the scope of your productized service is paramount. Clients should have a crystal-clear understanding of what is included and what is not. This clarity not only aids in effective communication but also minimizes potential misunderstandings. A well-defined scope lays the foundation for streamlined execution and client satisfaction.

**Strategic Pricing:**

Pricing your productized service demands a delicate balance between reflecting the value you provide and aligning with market expectations. Consider the perceived value of your standardized offering, taking into account the benefits it brings to clients. A strategic pricing structure should not only cover your costs but also position your service competitively in the market. Research your industry, analyze competitor pricing, and ensure that your rates are both reasonable and reflective of the quality you deliver.

**Value-Based Pricing:**

Value-based pricing is a potent strategy in productization. Instead of solely basing your pricing on the time or resources invested, consider the tangible value your service brings to clients. Highlight the outcomes, efficiencies, or solutions your productized service offers, anchoring your pricing in the perceived value rather than a simple cost-plus model.

**Adapting to Market Dynamics**:

Market dynamics play a crucial role in pricing strategies. Stay attuned to shifts in industry trends, client needs, and competitor pricing. Being adaptable allows you to tweak your pricing structure as needed, ensuring that your productized service remains competitive and appealing in a dynamic market landscape.

**Client-Centric Communication:**

Communicating your outlined service and pricing structure to potential clients is a pivotal aspect of this phase. Craft compelling messaging that not only highlights the features of your offering but also emphasizes the value clients will gain. Clear, transparent communication builds trust and establishes a solid foundation for long-term client relationships.

In essence, outlining and pricing your productized service are strategic endeavors that lay the groundwork for a successful side hustle. By creating a comprehensive outline, defining the scope with precision, and implementing a strategic pricing structure, you position your productized service for market success, ensuring that it not only meets but exceeds the expectations of your target audience.

## Real-World Examples of Successful Productized Services

Productizing services has become a transformative strategy for entrepreneurs, enabling them to scale their side hustles efficiently. Several real-world examples showcase the diversity and success of productized services across various industries, emphasizing the power of standardization and scalability.

**Online Courses Platforms:**

Platforms offering online courses exemplify the success of productization. Websites like Udemy, Teachable, and Skillshare provide instructors with the tools to create standardized courses that cater to a global audience. The courses, once developed, become products that can be accessed by countless users, showcasing the scalability inherent in productized services.

**Digital Marketing Agencies with Fixed Packages:**

In the realm of digital marketing, agencies that offer fixed packages for services like social media management, content creation, and SEO illustrate the power of productization. Clients can choose from predefined packages that align with their needs, streamlining the onboarding process and allowing agencies to efficiently serve a diverse clientele without the need for extensive customization.

**Website Development with Predefined Packages:**

Many website development agencies have embraced productization by offering predefined packages for services such as website design, development, and maintenance. Clients can select a package that aligns with their requirements, knowing exactly what they will receive for a set price. This model facilitates efficient project management and enables agencies to handle multiple clients simultaneously.

**Virtual Assistance Services:**

Virtual assistance services have successfully transitioned into productized offerings by providing predefined packages for tasks such as email management, scheduling, and research. Clients can choose a package that suits their needs, allowing virtual assistants to streamline their workflows and serve multiple clients with standardized services.

**Content Creation Subscriptions:**

Content creation services that offer subscription-based models for regular blog posts, social media content, or video production exemplify the subscription-based aspect of productization. Clients subscribe to receive a set amount of content regularly, providing a predictable income for the service provider and ensuring consistent delivery for the client.

These examples underscore the adaptability of productized services across diverse industries. Whether in education, marketing, web development, virtual assistance, or content creation, the common thread is the ability to standardize services into tangible products. The success of these real-world examples highlights the effectiveness of productization in meeting client needs, streamlining operations, and achieving scalability in the dynamic landscape of side hustles.

# Step 4: Recycle Your Money

## Reinvesting Profits: Fueling Growth and Expansion

In the evolution of a side hustle, Step 4 introduces a pivotal financial strategy—recycling your money by reinvesting profits back into the venture. This step is not just about accumulating wealth but strategically leveraging profits to fuel continuous growth, expand operations, and solidify the foundation for long-term success.

**Strategic Reinvestment:**

Reinvesting profits is akin to feeding the roots of a flourishing tree. Instead of immediately enjoying the fruits of success, this step involves redirecting earnings back into the side hustle. The objective is twofold: to enhance the existing infrastructure and to explore avenues for expansion. Strategic reinvestment becomes the lifeblood that nurtures sustained growth.

**Expanding Reach through Marketing:**

One key area for reinvestment is marketing. Allocating funds to marketing endeavors broadens the reach of the side hustle, attracting new clients or customers. Whether it's digital marketing campaigns, social media advertising, or other promotional activities, strategic reinvestment ensures that the side hustle remains visible in the competitive landscape.

**Investing in Equipment and Technology:**

Modern side hustles often rely on technology and specialized equipment. Reinvesting profits in upgraded tools, software, or machinery enhances efficiency, quality, and overall competitiveness. This proactive approach ensures that the side hustle stays at the forefront of industry standards, delivering optimal value to clients.

**Operational Efficiency and Automation:**

Reinvestment can also be directed towards optimizing operational efficiency through automation. Investing in software solutions, streamlined workflows, or outsourcing certain tasks can free up time and resources, allowing the side hustler to focus on strategic growth initiatives rather than getting bogged down in routine operations.

**Balancing Personal Wealth and Business Growth:**

While the temptation to enjoy personal luxuries may arise, it's crucial to strike a balance between personal financial goals and business growth. Taking some profits off the table to build personal wealth is important for financial security. Simultaneously, a portion of the profits should be earmarked for strategic reinvestment to ensure the continued expansion of the side hustle.

**The Safety Net of Diversification:**

In addition to internal reinvestment, diversifying investments can act as a safety net. Exploring opportunities outside the immediate side hustle, such as stock market investments or other ventures, provides a layer of financial security. This diversification shields against unforeseen challenges in the specific industry or market niche.

In essence, Step 4 represents the financial wisdom of recycling money within the side hustle ecosystem. By reinvesting profits strategically, entrepreneurs set the stage for not just financial success but sustained growth, operational efficiency, and resilience in the face of market dynamics. This step is the bridge between immediate gains and the creation of a robust, forward-looking side hustle.

# Strategic Spending vs. Impulsive Expenses

As a side hustle gains traction and begins generating profits, the critical choice between strategic spending and impulsive expenses emerges as a defining factor in its financial success. Strategic spending involves a deliberate and purposeful allocation of resources to areas that enhance growth, efficiency, and overall business sustainability. On the other hand, impulsive expenses are spontaneous, driven by momentary desires, and often lack a long-term strategic vision.

**Strategic Spending:**

Strategic spending is the cornerstone of financial intelligence in the context of a side hustle. It involves a meticulous examination of where funds can be most effectively deployed to foster growth and operational excellence. This may encompass investments in marketing, technology, skilled personnel, or other areas that directly contribute to the side hustle's competitiveness and market presence.

**Investing in Growth Initiatives:**

One aspect of strategic spending is investing in growth initiatives. This could entail expanding the product or service offering, entering new markets, or implementing marketing campaigns to attract a wider audience. By channeling resources into avenues that fuel expansion, strategic spending lays the groundwork for long-term success and revenue sustainability.

**Operational Efficiency and Technology:**

Strategic spending also extends to enhancing operational efficiency through the integration of technology and streamlined processes. Investing in tools, software, or automation solutions not only optimizes workflow but positions the side hustle as a tech-savvy player in the industry, contributing to overall competitiveness.

**Building a Resilient Infrastructure:**

Allocating funds to build a resilient infrastructure is another facet of strategic spending. This may involve creating backup systems, implementing risk management strategies, or developing contingency plans. Such investments fortify the side hustle against unforeseen challenges, contributing to its ability to weather market fluctuations.

**Impulsive Expenses:**

Contrastingly, impulsive expenses pose a potential threat to the financial health of a side hustle. These expenditures lack strategic intent and are often driven by momentary impulses, personal desires, or external pressures. Impulsive spending may include unnecessary luxuries, extravagant office spaces, or excessive personal withdrawals from the business funds.

**Balancing Immediate Gratification with Long-Term Vision:**

The challenge lies in striking a balance between immediate gratification and adherence to a long-term vision. While it's natural to enjoy the fruits of success, impulsive expenses can undermine the financial sustainability of the side hustle. Entrepreneurs must exercise discipline and discernment to differentiate between indulgence and investments that contribute to the venture's enduring success.

In conclusion, the dichotomy between strategic spending and impulsive expenses is a pivotal aspect of navigating the financial landscape of a side hustle. A commitment to strategic spending ensures that resources are directed purposefully, fostering growth and resilience. On the contrary, succumbing to impulsive expenses jeopardizes the financial stability and long-term viability of the side hustle. Making informed, strategic choices is the key to financial prosperity in the dynamic world of entrepreneurial endeavors.

## Building Personal Wealth: Investing in Stocks for Long-Term Financial Security

As a side hustle matures and begins to generate profits, the journey towards building personal wealth becomes a critical consideration. One strategic avenue for achieving long-term financial security is investing in stocks. While the side hustle thrives on active entrepreneurial efforts, investing in stocks offers a passive yet powerful mechanism to grow wealth over time.

### Stock Market as a Wealth-Building Tool:

Viewing the stock market as a wealth-building tool introduces a new dimension to personal financial strategies. Unlike the day-to-day dynamics of a side hustle, investing in stocks provides an opportunity for capital appreciation and wealth accumulation over the long term. Historically, the stock market has demonstrated the potential for average annual returns, making it a formidable avenue for wealth creation.

**Diversification and Risk Mitigation:**

Investing in a diversified portfolio of stocks serves as a risk mitigation strategy. Diversification involves spreading investments across different sectors, industries, and geographic regions. This approach minimizes the impact of poor-performing stocks on the overall portfolio. While the entrepreneurial landscape of a side hustle carries inherent risks, a diversified stock portfolio offers a level of risk management in the broader financial picture.

**Compounding Returns:**

The power of compounding returns is a compelling factor in stock market investing. Reinvesting dividends and allowing the investment to grow over time harnesses the compounding effect. This compounding leads to exponential growth, amplifying the initial investment and contributing significantly to long-term financial security.

**Passive Income through Dividends:**

Investing in dividend-paying stocks introduces an element of passive income. Dividend payments from well-established companies can serve as a consistent income stream, supplementing the earnings from the side hustle. This passive income contributes to financial stability and provides a cushion during economic downturns or periods of lower side hustle profitability.

**Long-Term Perspective and Patience:**

Successful stock market investing requires a long-term perspective and patience. Similarly, building personal wealth through stock investments aligns with a patient approach. While the side hustle demands active engagement and quick decision-making, the stock market rewards those who patiently weather short-term fluctuations with an eye on long-term goals.

**Balancing Act:**

The key lies in striking a balance between active entrepreneurship and the passive wealth-building potential of stocks. Allocating a portion of the profits generated by the side hustle to stock investments creates a harmonious synergy between the dynamic, hands-on nature of the entrepreneurial venture and the stable, long-term growth potential offered by the stock market.

In conclusion, building personal wealth through stock market investments complements the active efforts of a side hustle, providing a pathway to long-term financial security. By embracing the principles of diversification, compounding returns, and a patient outlook, entrepreneurs can navigate the dynamic financial landscape with a comprehensive strategy that combines entrepreneurial vigor with the steady growth afforded by the stock market.

# Step 5: Automate Everything - Transitioning from a Profitable Job to a Sustainable Side Hustle

Step 5 marks the pinnacle of entrepreneurial evolution—the transition from a profitable job to a sustainable side hustle achieved through the strategic implementation of automation. This transformative step involves unlocking the special moves and cheat codes of the business world, liberating entrepreneurs from the constraints of conventional rules and propelling their ventures into a realm of efficiency, scalability, and sustained success.

**The Essence of Automation:**

Automation is the secret sauce that propels a side hustle beyond the realm of a profitable job. It involves streamlining processes, delegating tasks, and harnessing technology to handle routine operations. The essence lies in freeing up valuable time and mental bandwidth, allowing entrepreneurs to focus on strategic growth initiatives rather than getting bogged down in day-to-day minutiae.

**Unlocking Special Moves:**

Transitioning from a profitable job to a sustainable side hustle is akin to unlocking special moves in the entrepreneurial game. Automation empowers entrepreneurs to transcend the limitations of time and resources, enabling them to scale their ventures exponentially. Tasks that were once manually intensive can now be executed seamlessly through automated systems, paving the way for increased efficiency and productivity.

**Efficiency Through Delegation:**

Delegating responsibilities is a key component of automation. Entrepreneurs can strategically assign tasks to capable team members, virtual assistants, or automated tools, ensuring that the side hustle operates like a well-oiled machine. This not only enhances efficiency but also positions the venture for scalability without overwhelming the entrepreneur.

**Strategic Focus on Growth:**

With automation handling routine tasks, entrepreneurs can redirect their focus toward strategic growth initiatives. Whether it's expanding product lines, entering new markets, or innovating within the industry, the newfound freedom allows for a visionary approach to steering the side hustle towards sustained success.

**Avoiding the Pitfall of Selfish Tendencies:**

Despite the advantages of automation, entrepreneurs must guard against succumbing to selfish tendencies that resist delegation. The temptation to retain control over every aspect of the side hustle can impede progress. Recognizing the bigger picture—building an automated machine that is the side hustle—is crucial in overcoming these tendencies.

**The Rich and Powerful Understand Automation:**

A profound understanding of automation sets the rich and powerful apart from the average entrepreneur. The ability to transcend the limitations of a profitable job and build a sustainable, automated side hustle is a hallmark of those who live a fundamentally different life. It's a recognition that time is the ultimate currency, and automating routine tasks is the key to unlocking its full potential.

In conclusion, Step 5 marks the liberation of entrepreneurs from the confines of a profitable job, ushering them into the realm of a sustainable, automated side hustle. This transition involves leveraging technology, streamlining processes, and strategically delegating responsibilities to unlock the special moves that propel the venture into a league of its own. Automation is not just a business strategy; it's the ultimate game-changer in the journey towards sustained entrepreneurial success.

## Building a Team: Handing Over Responsibilities

As a side hustle matures and strives for sustained success, the strategic move of building a team becomes imperative. The entrepreneurial journey evolves from a solo venture to a collaborative effort, with the crucial step of handing over responsibilities to a capable team. This transformative process is not just about delegation; it's a strategic maneuver to amplify efficiency, foster specialization, and elevate the side hustle to new heights.

**Recognizing the Limitations of Solo Endeavors:**

Solo entrepreneurship can only go so far. Recognizing the limitations of a one-person show is the catalyst for building a team. While the initial stages of a side hustle often require a hands-on approach, growth demands a collective effort. The entrepreneur acknowledges that to achieve more, they need a team with diverse skills and perspectives.

**Strategic Delegation:**

Handing over responsibilities is more than mere delegation; it's a strategic act. Entrepreneurs identify their strengths and areas of expertise, then strategically delegate tasks that align with the strengths of team members. This not only accelerates task completion but ensures that each aspect of the business is handled by individuals with the most relevant skills.

**Efficiency Through Specialization:**

Building a team allows for specialization, where team members excel in specific areas of expertise. Instead of being a jack of all trades, the entrepreneur becomes the orchestrator, ensuring that each team member contributes their specialized skills to the overall success of the side hustle. This efficiency through specialization is a cornerstone of a high-functioning team.

**Cultivating a Collaborative Culture:**

A successful team is not just a collection of individuals but a cohesive unit with a shared vision. Entrepreneurs actively cultivate a collaborative culture, fostering open communication, shared goals, and a sense of ownership among team members. This collaborative environment becomes the bedrock for innovation and sustained growth.

**Elevating the Side Hustle to New Heights:**

Handing over responsibilities is the catalyst for elevating the side hustle to new heights. With a well-functioning team, the entrepreneur is no longer constrained by the limitations of time and individual capacity. The collective energy and expertise propel the side hustle beyond what a solo endeavor could achieve, opening doors to scalability and expanded opportunities.

**Overcoming the Fear of Letting Go:**

For many entrepreneurs, handing over responsibilities is accompanied by a fear of letting go. However, overcoming this fear is essential for growth. Trusting in the capabilities of the team, providing clear guidelines, and fostering a culture of accountability are crucial steps in navigating this shift from a solo venture to a team-driven enterprise.

In conclusion, building a team and handing over responsibilities is a pivotal phase in the entrepreneurial journey. It's a strategic move that transcends the constraints of solo endeavors, unlocking the full potential of the side hustle. Through efficient delegation, specialization, and a collaborative culture, entrepreneurs pave the way for sustained success and the realization of broader business objectives.

## The Bigger Picture: Creating an Automated Machine for Lasting Success

As entrepreneurs embark on the journey of turning a profitable job into a sustainable side hustle, the concept of the bigger picture takes center stage. The ultimate goal transcends immediate gains and involves creating an automated machine that operates seamlessly, paving the way for lasting success. This visionary approach is not just about the daily operations of the side hustle but encompasses strategic planning, scalability, and a legacy mindset.

**Beyond Immediate Profits:**

The quest for the bigger picture requires entrepreneurs to look beyond immediate profits and envision the long-term trajectory of their side hustle. It involves a shift from a transactional mindset to a strategic one, where every decision is guided by the question of how it contributes to the enduring success of the venture.

**Strategic Planning for Scalability:**

Creating an automated machine necessitates strategic planning for scalability. Entrepreneurs map out the growth trajectory of their side hustle, identifying potential challenges and opportunities. This forward-thinking approach ensures that the side hustle is not just profitable today but has the infrastructure to adapt and thrive in a changing business landscape.

**Legacy Mindset:**

The bigger picture involves cultivating a legacy mindset. Entrepreneurs aspire to leave a lasting impact, not just as individuals but as creators of a sustainable enterprise. This mindset influences decisions, encouraging a focus on building processes, systems, and a team that can carry the side hustle forward even in the absence of direct involvement.

**Efficiency through Automation:**

Automation becomes a cornerstone in painting the bigger picture. Entrepreneurs strategically implement automated systems for routine tasks, freeing up time and resources. This efficiency allows for a more profound focus on strategic initiatives that contribute to the long-term success of the side hustle.

**Balancing Short-Term Gains and Long-Term Vision:**

Navigating the journey of creating an automated machine requires a delicate balance between short-term gains and long-term vision. While immediate profits are essential for sustaining the side hustle, they are viewed as stepping stones towards the grander vision of a self-sustaining, automated entity.

**Continued Adaptation and Innovation:**

The bigger picture acknowledges the dynamic nature of business environments. Entrepreneurs commit to continued adaptation and innovation, ensuring that the automated machine remains relevant and competitive. This commitment to evolution positions the side hustle as a resilient force in the ever-changing marketplace.

In conclusion, creating an automated machine for lasting success is the culmination of an entrepreneurial evolution. It involves thinking beyond the confines of daily operations and envisioning a legacy of sustained impact. By strategically planning for scalability, embracing a legacy mindset, and leveraging automation, entrepreneurs not only secure the success of their side hustle today but lay the groundwork for a thriving and enduring enterprise in the future.

# Conclusion

In the dynamic landscape of side hustles, this journey has unraveled the intricacies of transforming a profitable endeavor into a sustainable, automated machine for enduring success. From dispelling common myths surrounding entrepreneurship to the strategic steps of developing skills, offering standout services, productizing offerings, recycling profits, and ultimately automating processes, each chapter has been a stepping stone toward the bigger picture.

The entrepreneurial path is not just about immediate gains; it's a visionary quest to build a legacy. As we conclude this exploration, remember that the journey is a dynamic interplay between strategic thinking, delegation, and embracing the transformative power of automation. It's a journey that demands a shift from being a sole contributor to orchestrating a collaborative team, from a profitable job to a side hustle that thrives independently.

The key lies in understanding that success is not a sprint but a marathon. By adopting a legacy mindset, planning for scalability, and integrating automation, entrepreneurs can create a side hustle that not only survives but thrives in the ever-evolving business landscape. As you embark on your own entrepreneurial odyssey, keep the bigger picture in focus – the creation of an automated machine that stands the test of time, leaving an indelible mark on the world of side hustles. May your journey be marked by innovation, resilience, and the realization of lasting success.

www.ingramcontent.com/pod-product-compliance
Lightning Source LLC
Chambersburg PA
CBHW060211260726
48658CB00005BA/1989